SNAKE CHARMER

for Mooljee and Dhanlaxmi Nagda

Henry Holt and Company, LLC, Publishers since 1866
115 West 18th Street, New York, New York 10011
Henry Holt is a registered trademark of Henry Holt and Company, LLC

Library of Congress Cataloging-in-Publication Data
Nagda, Ann Whitehead.
Snake charmer / by Ann Whitehead Nagda.
1. Snake charmers—India—Juvenile literature. 2. Occupations—India—Juvenile literature.
[1. Snake charmers—India. 2. Occupations. 3. India—Social life and customs.] 1. Title.
GV1831.S6N34 2002 791.8—dc21 2001016967

ISBN 0-8050-6499-0 / First Edition—2002
Printed in the United States of America on acid-free paper. ∞
Designed by Meredith Pratt

10 9 8 7 6 5 4 3 2 1

All photographs were taken by Ann Whitehead Nagda with the following exceptions: Jagdish M. Nagda,
page 8, and Joyce Gellhorn, pages 9 (both), 17, 21, 22, 30.

S·N·A·K·E CHARMER

by Ann Whitehead Nagda

Henry Holt and Company
New York

The high sweet sound of a flute wafts over the village.

Children race down dusty streets to join the growing crowd. A man in a bright yellow shirt sits in front of a round covered basket. He raps sharply on the basket, then lifts the lid. A cobra rears up, spreading its hood. The man plays his flute, swaying his body back and forth. The snake sways too, its black eyes fixed on the man and his flute. On the back of the snake's hood, two bright markings that look like eyes seem to stare at the audience. The snake is an Indian spectacled cobra. The flute player is Sher Singh, a snake charmer who lives in northern India.

The art of snake charming is passed down from father to son. Sher Singh learned all about snakes from his father, Narwar Nath.

Vishnu, Sher Singh's oldest son, wants to be a snake charmer too. He'd like a cobra of his own, one that will rise from a basket while he plays the flute.

Vishnu dreams of going to Agra. That's where Sher Singh and Narwar Nath live and perform during the seven months of the year when tourists visit India. Vishnu wants to see the historic buildings he's heard so much about. He wants to go to the movies and wander through stores that sell toys.

Most of all, he'd like to help his father and grandfather with the cobras, rat snakes, sand boas, and the one large python. But Vishnu's father says school is more important.

So Vishnu stays home in Mania, but he looks forward to spending time with his father. Every two weeks, Sher Singh and Narwar Nath pack up their snakes and return home for a short visit. They ride their bicycles along highways where trucks and buses speed past bullock carts loaded with sugarcane.

Vishnu has ridden around his village on the back of his father's bike, so he knows the dangers of Indian roads. There are large potholes, and cows sometimes wander into the traffic.

Every day after school, Vishnu plays marbles with his
friends. His little brother, Tej, always begs to join in.
Today their father rides into the village on his big
black bike, so Vishnu leaves the game and runs to say
hello. Bhudevi, his mother, serves her husband water
from a brass jug, then she makes the evening meal of
rice and curried vegetables.

Puja, Vishnu's younger sister, often helps their mother care for baby Ruby. Sometimes his older sister, Hemlata, helps too.

In the evening, the oil lamp is lit, and Vishnu sits with his family for story time.

The village doesn't have electricity, so there is no TV. The adults tell folktales that show how people are related to the world around them. The moon is their sister, the trees are their brothers, and all animals are their cousins.

At night the family sleeps together in their one-room brick house. Vishnu and his brother and sisters sleep on quilts on the floor. His parents sleep on woven mats attached to wooden bed frames. The snakes sleep in their baskets, which are stored under the beds. Vishnu's grandparents sleep in their own house.

Vishnu's mother gets up just as the sun is rising. The air is still cool. She feeds the baby, sweeps the house, gives the cow some hay, fetches water from the well, and grinds grain into flour with a stone grinder.

Finally, she starts a fire and cooks chapatis, a flat bread made from flour and water. Vishnu and his family have their breakfast of bread and tea.

After breakfast, the village boys take baths by the well. The water is cold. A woman pumps water for cooking. An old man brings his cow for a drink.

Vishnu helps with some of the household chores. He and Tej collect firewood and cow dung. Bhudevi mixes the dung with straw. Hemlata helps her mother shape the mixture into flat round cakes. When the cakes are dry, they are used to make cooking fires. Bhudevi also spreads cow dung on the floor of the house, where it hardens like concrete.

Once the milkman has come, Vishnu helps his father feed the snakes. Sher Singh pours milk into a shallow pan. He takes a cobra from a basket and holds its face in the milk. The cobra hisses and tries to strike his arm.

According to Indian folklore, snakes like milk, although this particular snake doesn't seem interested. Vishnu watches his father feed milk to a baby sand boa. He can hardly believe that this tiny snake, not much larger than a worm, will grow to be three feet long.

Later, Vishnu follows his father into the nearby fields to hunt for more snakes. When Sher Singh captures a snake he always makes a promise to let it go some day. Last night he released one of his rat snakes and now he must capture another one.

He leads his son through a wheat field. Vishnu points to snake tracks in the dirt. Sher Singh shows his son a hole at the base of a tree. It's the entrance to a rat's burrow. He enlarges the hole with his snake stick. Now Vishnu can see the big coiled snake.

Sher Singh pulls it from the hole using the snake stick, then grabs it behind its head. Vishnu takes the rat snake, which is not poisonous. He dreams of finding a cobra, but Sher Singh says that cobras are too dangerous for young boys.

Vishnu is disappointed, but he still likes playing with the rat snake. It wraps its tail around his arm. Its forked tongue darts in and out. The snake bites Vishnu's hand, but the bite doesn't hurt too much.

Narwar Nath lets Vishnu feed a mango to his mongoose. Vishnu wants to see the mongoose fight a cobra. His grandfather takes a cobra from its basket. It rises and spreads its hood. The mongoose tries to bite the snake's neck, but it hisses and strikes. The mongoose jumps away and tries again from a different direction. Vishnu pulls the mongoose away before it can hurt the cobra. He pats the fearless little animal and gives it a piece of chocolate. His grandfather laughs and says the mongoose will eat anything.

Late in the afternoon, Sher Singh and Vishnu sit with
their neighbors in the cool shade of a tree in the village
square. Sher Singh uses beeswax to glue a bamboo pipe
and a brass pipe to a gourd to make a snake flute. When
it is finished, Vishnu brings a snake basket from the
house. Children gather to watch. Sher Singh plays the
flute and sways back and forth, and the two cobras sway
too. Vishnu knows they are following the movement of
the flute because they think the flute might be an enemy.

Vishnu would like to try
the new flute, but his father
hands it to Tej instead.

Tej doesn't play very well—only high-pitched squeaks
come out. He stops playing, and the cobras glide into
the crowd. Everyone laughs. Vishnu knows his father
has removed the poison glands, so the cobras can't hurt
anyone. He picks up the snakes and puts them back in
the basket.

Early the next morning, Vishnu's father pumps up the tires on his bicycle before returning to Agra. As always, Vishnu asks if he can go with his father and help with the snakes. But Sher Singh says no. The government has turned against snake charmers. Too many snakes were being killed to make wallets and purses and belts. Sometimes wildlife officials take snakes away from snake charmers. Sher Singh wants Vishnu to have a better job.

After his father leaves, Vishnu walks to the village school with Tej, Puja, and Hemlata.

He sits outside and practices writing numbers on his slate with chalk. Birds twitter in the tree above him. A cool breeze tickles his skin.

Sometimes Vishnu asks Hemlata to help him read. She is twelve and spends her school days indoors with the older children. Hemlata has learned to read Hindi and has begun to learn English. Neither their mother nor their father can read or write.

Vishnu knows these are important skills that he will need in the future. With the help of his sister and his teachers, he will learn to read. Someday Vishnu wants to get a job that will make his father proud. But he will always dream about charming snakes.

About Snake Charmers and Their Snakes

People have been charming snakes since at least 300 B.C. The practice may have originated in India or Egypt, but today snake charmers can be found throughout southern Asia and northern Africa. In India alone, there are half a million snake charmers.

Snake charming is not just fun to watch: it's a good way to remove snakes from houses without harming the animals. In India, snakes are considered holy and killing them would be unthinkable, yet they are responsible for the deaths of at least thirty thousand people every year. Millions of people live near areas where poisonous snakes search for food. These snakes often enter homes to get away from the heat or because the fields or rat burrows where they live have been flooded by monsoon rains.

A boy can start training to be a snake charmer when he is five or six years old. At first he learns to handle nonpoisonous snakes, like the gentle-natured rat snake. Then his father teaches him how to catch and care for snakes. The boy must also learn to identify the different kinds of snakes and understand their habits. He spends lots of time practicing on the bheen, or snake flute. By the time the boy is twelve years old, he is ready to give shows at local festivals or at tourist attractions in the larger cities.

Snake charmers use cobras in their shows because of the way these snakes react when they feel threatened. Cobras raise the front part of their bodies and spread the ribs of their necks to form hoods, which makes them look bigger than they actually are. It's not the flute's music that makes cobras respond this way—they can barely hear. It is the movement of the flute that makes them feel threatened. Cobras are timid snakes that would rather hide than fight. They are also very sensitive and will often refuse to eat in captivity. In the wild, cobras eat rats, mice, frogs, lizards, and other snakes.

There are myths from all over the world about offering milk to snakes. In one Indian folktale, a mother cobra is very angry when a farmer accidentally kills her three babies. The farmer's daughter saves her family from the mother cobra's revenge by giving her a bowl of milk. Snakes are not normally interested in milk unless they are very thirsty, but snake charmers still offer it to them. They also offer them bits of meat, insects, mice, and lizards.

Cobras and rat snakes both take over the burrows of rats or other rodents. Snake charmers know to look for snakes in these burrows. Often there are dikes, or mounds of dirt, separating two fields, and rodents nest in these dikes. Rats are a big problem for farmers because they eat the grain ripening in the fields. Snakes eat rats and mice so they are important to farmers. In the 1960s and 1970s, when millions of snakes in India were killed to make leather goods, there were major rodent outbreaks.

Today the Indian government tries to protect snakes. There are laws that limit the export of live snakes or their skins. Everyone who catches snakes must have a capture license. But making people obey these laws is difficult in a country with one billion people. Sher Singh says there are eight or ten men in his village who still practice snake charming. Like Sher Singh, they are poor and illiterate men with no training to do anything else. If wildlife officials were to come and take their snakes, they would simply catch some more. Sher Singh says that even if he were no longer a snake charmer, he would still feel great affection for the snakes that live around him. And his children will always think of snakes as their friends.